HERE I AM
TO
WORSHIP
DEVOTIONAL

Devotions Inspired by the Song

HONOR [HB] BOOKS

Inspiration and Motivation for the Season of Life

COOK COMMUNICATIONS MINISTRIES
Colorado Springs, Colorado • Paris, Ontario
KINGSWAY COMMUNICATIONS LTD
Eastbourne, England

Honor® is an imprint of
Cook Communications Ministries, Colorado Springs, CO 80918
Cook Communications, Paris, Ontario
Kingsway Communications, Eastbourne, England

HERE I AM TO WORSHIP
© 2005 by Cook Communications Ministries

Cover Design: BMB Design/Scott Johnson

First Printing, 2005
Printed in Canada

     1 2 3 4 5 6 7 8 9 10 Printing/Year 10 09 08 07 06 05

Library of Congress Cataloging-in-Publication Data

Palmer, Adam, 1975-
  Here I am to worship : devotions inspired by the song / [Adam
Palmer].
      p. cm. -- (30 days of worship)
  ISBN 1-56292-716-7
 1. Hymns--Devotional use. 2. Devotional calendars. I. Title. II.
Series.
  BV340.P35 2005

                                        2005020789

Introduction

Worship songs have become the anthems of modern Christianity. They unite us in a unique way, a way that other portions of church services never will. Though we don't all attend the same church, hear the same sermons, or share the same theology, most Christians can find praise and worship music they love. It is a small part of our shared Christian experience—appreciation for a certain lyric or part of the music. We may sing them differently, but we sing the same songs.

Such is the case with "Here I Am to Worship." Written by Tim Hughes, the song is a humble cry to God, a simple way of stating, over and over again, where our allegiances lie. It is simply a musical way of reminding ourselves—and God—of his importance in our lives.

What follows is a simple, easy-to-read devotional, designed to delve into the themes of "Here I Am to Worship" over the course of thirty days. Each day focuses on a different part of the song, examining it under a microscope to uncover the life-applicable truths it contains.

May you find revelation and comfort within these pages. And may you come to know God in a deeper way as you prayerfully consider why and whom you are here to worship.

Here I Am to Worship

BY TIM HUGHES

Light of the world
You stepped down into darkness
Opened my eyes let me see
Beauty that made this heart adore You
Hope of a life spent with You

Here I am to worship
Here I am to bow down
Here I am to say that You're my God
You're altogether lovely
Altogether worthy
Altogether wonderful to me

King of all days
Oh so highly exalted
Glorious in Heaven above
Humbly You came to the earth You created
All for love's sake became poor

I'll never know how much it cost
To see my sin upon that cross

DAY 1: Light of the World

When Jesus spoke again to the people, he said, "I am the light of the world. Whoever follows me will never walk in darkness, but will have the light of life."

—JOHN 8:12

Worship involves following.

Whose lead do you follow? When you worship at church, you follow the worship leader. When you listen to the sermon, you follow your pastor. When you leave, you probably follow the car in front of you.

But who do you follow?

Jesus said he is light in this dark world, and if we get tired of the darkness—which we should—we only need to follow him to live a life of walking in the light.

Walking in the dark is most certainly not easy. Even in your own home, where you may know the layout like the back of your hand, pitfalls abound. How many times have you stubbed your toe while heading to the bathroom in the middle of the night? How many times have you stepped on something you'd forgotten was on the floor? Can you imagine living your entire life that way, walking through a spiritual darkness?

We must turn on the light. We must follow Jesus. Wherever he may lead us.

That can be a scary thought, especially since he may not illuminate the entire path we're walking. We may only get a glimpse or two of the direction we're headed, but as long as we stick close to Jesus, the light of the world, we'll be able to see what he needs and wants us to see.

**He is the light of the world.
Follow him out of darkness and
gain the light of life.**

Prayer for the Day:

Lord, I repent of the times I choose to stay in my darkness. I want to live as close to your light as possible. Give me the strength, the courage, and the wisdom to follow you as you light my way. Please help me stay close to you as I follow, so that my entire life journey may glorify you. Please use my life as a reflection of your light that will shine on others. I worship you, Jesus, light of the world.

AMEN.

DAY 2: Light of the World

The LORD reigns, let the earth be glad; let the distant shores rejoice.... His lightning lights up the world; the earth sees and trembles. The mountains melt like wax before the LORD, before the Lord of all the earth. The heavens proclaim his righteousness, and all the peoples see his glory.

—PSALM 97:1, 4–6

Worship involves the Almighty God.

Think about the sun for a moment, the practical light of our particular world. It is a nonstop nuclear reactor, generating millions of degrees of heat. It is also enormous: If it were hollow, more than one million earths would fit inside it. It lies 93 million miles away from earth, a considerable distance, yet it generates so much heat that even with the buffer of earth's atmosphere, direct sunlight can be scorchingly unbearable in certain places.

The sun is impressive. And God dwarfs it.

God is Almighty. He created the sun, the moon, the stars, and this very planet we live on. And all of his creation sings to him; each blade of grass, each grain of sand, each particle of space dust—it all proclaims God's glory and righteousness.

Our attempts at lighting our world are feeble at best and are always impermanent. They also rely on the resources God himself created. Light bulbs, fireplaces, flashlights—these are the ways we try to light our world. Generously compared to the sun, they are but a mere flicker, but they are the best we can do in our extremely limited capacity.

We are weak, but God is strong.
And he allows us the opportunity
to approach him in worship.

Amazing.

Prayer for the Day:

Lord, help me to grasp your awesome light in even the slightest way. Help me, Lord, to respond to you in an appropriate way today. Help me to see your creativity and imagination as I walk through the world you've created, the world you light up so brilliantly. I stand in awe of you, God.

AMEN.

DAY 3:
You Stepped Down into Darkness

In the beginning God created the heavens and the earth. Now the earth was formless and empty, darkness was over the surface of the deep, and the Spirit of God was hovering over the waters.

—GENESIS 1:1–2

Worship involves openness to God's light.

Darkness has no power of its own. Scientists will never be able to counteract the power of light by inventing a dark bulb that spreads darkness when it's turned on. Campers will never use flashdarks, cars will never have head-darks.

Darkness isn't really darkness—it is the absence of light. Darkness is defined by light. Light is not defined by darkness, light rules over darkness.

The world was dark at the beginning because it had nothing. Then God stepped in with four simple words: "Let there be light." And suddenly the darkness could define itself because it had finally met the very thing that defined it.

This is why our hearts crave the light of the Lord. Our hearts are dark places, made dark by the absence of Christ's light. Our sin nature revels in this darkness, for it is only in darkness that it is allowed to operate unchecked.

When we worship with openness, we expose our dark places to God. We say, "God, come step into our personal darkness so that you can create something wonderful and beautiful." This world we live in began when God stepped down into darkness and brought his light.

Our world begins the same way, with God stepping into our darkness. But we must let him.

Prayer for the Day:

Lord, define my life with your light. I offer every part of my darkness to you; please shine your light on all the hidden corners of my heart that I didn't even know were there. God, let your light flood into my heart as you step down into my darkness. I open myself to your light. I love you, Lord, and I want to worship you with every part of me.

AMEN.

DAY 4:
You Stepped Down into Darkness

*For God so loved the world that he gave his one and only
Son, that whoever believes in him shall not perish but have*

eternal life. For God did not send his Son into the world to condemn the world, but to save the world through him. Whoever believes in him is not condemned, but whoever does not believe stands condemned already because he has not believed in the name of God's one and only Son. This is the verdict: Light has come into the world, but men loved darkness instead of light because their deeds were evil.

—JOHN 3:16–19

Worship involves the acceptance of Jesus' work on the cross.

The world was physically dark before God created it. It was spiritually dark before God redeemed it. God sent his son as a way to dissipate the darkness that surrounds each and every one of us—the darkness of evil deeds, the darkness of selfish ambitions, the darkness of greed, jealousy, lust, hatred, racism ... the darkness of mankind.

But in order for that darkness to vanish, we must accept the work that Jesus did when he came into this world. Because God knew we'd never be able to light our own way, he sent Jesus. God stepped into this darkness once when he spoke creation into being, but then he stepped into it again—in human form—when he sent Jesus.

And he did it for love.

There are people today who can look at that act of love and turn their backs on it, because they love their evil deeds more than they love Jesus' sacrifice. But when we worship Jesus for stepping into our darkness, we turn fully toward that act of love and embrace it. When we accept Jesus' sacrifice and his work, we are inviting him to step into our darkness. We are showing that we love him more than we love evil deeds, to the point of exposing those deeds to the light.

The evil darkness cannot withstand the truth of Jesus' light.

Prayer for the Day:

I worship you, Jesus, for choosing the cross and stepping into my darkness. I praise you for accepting the task of sacrificing your life so that I can walk in the light, and I accept your sacrifice. Help me live a life of light this day, so that I may honor your sacrifice and worship you with good deeds instead of evil deeds. I love you, Lord.

AMEN.

DAY 5:
Opened
My Eyes
Let Me
See

But whoever lives by the truth comes into the light, so that it may be seen plainly that what he has done has been done through God.

—JOHN 3:21

Worship involves reliance on God.

Imagine a car that suddenly becomes aware of its surroundings. It is parked in a garage. As it looks around, it thinks to itself, "This is a nice garage I've driven myself to. There's plenty of oil over there on that shelf, and I can tell this is a clean place. Yes, I've done a good thing and brought myself to this garage."

The car is, of course, fooling itself. It has been driven to the garage by its owner, and it has been driven there for the express purpose of having its engine removed and replaced. If it were to think to itself, "I'll be leaving now," it would have absolutely no means of doing so.

We are the same way. We can take a look at our station in life and pat ourselves on the backs for the great job we did in getting where we are today, but if we do so, we are fooling ourselves. For we are not looking with eyes that God has opened.

If we look with those God-opened eyes, we begin to see ourselves as we are—capable of doing nothing except through God. We aren't doing anything on our own, but we can plainly see that what we do, we do through God's help.

He is both the driver and the engine of our individual cars.

Prayer for the Day:

Lord, forgive me for the times I forget that I rely on you and only you to accomplish the things I must do. Help me to remember it is your hand that's guiding me, and help me to listen to your voice so that I may continue to rely on you. Give me open eyes, Lord, so that I may see your direction and follow it plainly. I worship you with open eyes.

AMEN.

DAY 6: Opened My Eyes Let Me See

When the servant of the man of God got up and went out early the next morning, an army with horses and chariots had surrounded the city. "Oh, my lord, what shall we do?" the servant asked. "Don't be afraid," the prophet answered. "Those who are with us are more than those who are with them." And Elisha prayed, "O Lord, open his eyes so he may see." Then the Lord opened the servant's eyes, and he looked and saw the hills full of horses and chariots of fire all around Elisha.

—2 Kings 6:15–17

Worship involves perspective.

Our eyes often deceive us. On a hot, humid day, we can look down a long road and see what appears to be a shimmering pool of water—but it is only a mirage. We can see a magician and be amazed at his tricks—but he is only fooling our eyes.

But seeing with God's eyes is an entirely different notion. Gehazi, the "servant of the man of God" referenced in today's passage of scripture, began the passage looking through his natural eyes, eyes that were easily deceived. With that perspective, Gehazi began to worry for his and Elisha's safety.

But after Elisha prayed, Gehazi received truly open eyes, and his fears were put to rest as he saw the situation from God's perspective. He now saw that being afraid of the natural armies that surrounded him was an errant perspective. Because he saw the situation as God saw it, he recognized that the enemy armies were the ones in trouble, not him.

When we worship, we're asking God to open our eyes so that we may truly see a situation from his perspective. Though we may be tempted to be weighed down by the armies of evil that surround us, God lifts that weight by showing us the world as he sees it. God is on our side, and he gives us the proper perspective.

He is in charge.
Our eyes are open.

Prayer for the Day:

Lord, open my eyes. I recognize that I cannot see the whole picture the same way that you see it, so please allow me to glimpse things the way you see them. Give me your perspective on my life so that I may follow you with abandon and share that perspective with everyone I encounter today. I thank you, Lord, for open eyes, and I worship you with those eyes wide open.

AMEN.

DAY 7: Beauty That Made This Heart Adore You

While he was in Bethany, reclining at the table in the home of a man known as Simon the Leper, a woman came with an alabaster jar of very expensive perfume, made of pure nard. She broke the jar and poured the perfume on his head. Some of those present were saying indignantly to one another, "Why this waste of perfume? It could have been sold for more than a year's wages and the money given to the poor." And they rebuked her harshly. "Leave her alone," said Jesus. "Why are you bothering her? She has done a beautiful thing to me. The poor you will always have with you, and you can help them any time you want. But you will not always have me. She did what she could. She poured perfume on my body beforehand to prepare for my burial. I tell you the truth, wherever the gospel is preached throughout the world, what she has done will also be told, in memory of her."

—MARK 14:3–9

Worship involves wholehearted participation.

What a beautiful gesture. This woman of ill repute came to Jesus and lavished a gift upon him as her way of worshiping him. It's almost as if this woman understood the nature of Jesus' mission on earth before anyone else: He was about to give his life—his all—for mankind. The least she could do was lavish Jesus with this extravagant gesture of love and worship.

Extravagance is never wasted on God. There is no way we can push him to the point of saying, "Okay, enough already! I believe that you love me! Give it a rest and go watch TV or something." On the contrary, God revels in our wholehearted adoration.

When we worship God with our whole hearts, with everything in us, we are, in a sense, reenacting this woman's extravagant gift.

We mustn't be afraid to break open our jars of expensive perfume—the things we hold most dear—and offer them to Jesus. Though we may feel like we are losing something, we are indeed gaining the whole world.

We please God when we worship him without reservation.

Prayer for the Day:

Lord, here they are. Here are the things I treasure. The pastimes I love, the people I adore, the activities I crave—I present them all to you. It is all I can do. I pray that you will let me continue to love you with my whole heart, with no reservation, holding nothing back. I worship you with abandon, Jesus.

AMEN.

DAY 8:
Beauty That Made This Heart Adore You

In my Father's house are many rooms; if it were not so, I would have told you. I am going there to prepare a place for you. And if I go and prepare a place for you, I will come back and take you to be with me that you also may be where I am.

—JOHN 14:2–3

Worship involves eternity.

What a wonderful hope! Our hearts yearn for eternity because our hearts were made for eternity. And it is there—in eternity—that we will see the fruition of our deepest dreams and desires—an unending amount of time to spend with God.

Is there anything in this world you can imagine that has no ending? Everything in our lives is finite—every single thing we encounter every single second of the day will someday end. Even the seemingly endless expanse of space has an ending.

So it is difficult for us to wrap our minds around an eternity—a never-ending time— spent with a God we've never seen face to face. Yet it should thrill us to ponder it. We have a better future for a better life.

This is our hope. On our worst days, on our best days—there is no hope that will ever outlast or outweigh the hope of eternity. It is the greatest thing we can hope for, and we can get the tiniest taste of it when we set our face toward him and reflect on that hope.

We can taste the eternity that awaits us when we worship him.

Prayer for the Day:

Dear heavenly Father, I am amazed that you chose me as one of the souls to spend eternity with you. I am humbled and awed at the hope of eternity that you've given my heart. As I live my life this day, please use that hope to guide me in all my actions and all my decisions. Remind me that my choices this day can and will have ramifications in eternity. I can't wait to see you face to face, God. I long for eternity with you.

AMEN.

DAY 9: Hope of a Life Spent with You

One thing I ask of the Lord, this is what I seek: that I may dwell in the house of the Lord all the days of my life, to gaze upon the beauty of the Lord and to seek him in his temple.

—Psalm 27:4

Worship involves time.

We are incapable of comprehending God's beauty. David wrote this psalm with the desire that he could spend his lifetime gazing on God's beauty—perhaps because he somewhat understood that it would take a lifetime to even begin comprehending it.

Those of us who are married have already begun to experience this. No matter how much we know about our spouses, there's always something new to discover. Each new year brings new discoveries about them that we hadn't known before. However, there is no possible way we can ever fully know our spouses as well as we know ourselves.

It is the same way with God.

We can never fully know him. And yet, our innermost desire is to do just that—to know him. Which is why we are called to seek him.

Day after glorious day, our soul desires to know God more and more. To seek after him each day so that his beauty can enthrall our hearts ever further, so that our hope for eternity can grow ever greater.

And so we seek him. Not out of futility, but because there can be no greater honor than seeking after the beauty of God's face, longing to gaze upon it forever and ever.

Prayer for the Day:

O Lord, you're beautiful. I pray that you'll allow me the honor of seeking you daily, so that I may see your beauty. Show me your beauty in your creation. Show me your beauty in other people. Show me your beauty, Jesus, through the sacrifice you made on the cross. I adore you, Lord, and I thank you for letting me seek you.

AMEN.

DAY 10:
Here I Am to Worship

Now Moses was tending the flock of Jethro his father-in-law, the priest of Midian, and he led the flock to the far side of the desert and came to Horeb, the mountain of God. There the angel of the LORD appeared to him in flames of fire from within a bush. Moses saw that though the bush was on fire it did not burn up. So Moses thought, "I will go over and see this strange sight—why the bush does not burn up." When the LORD saw that he had gone over to look, God called to him from within the bush, "Moses! Moses!" And Moses said, "Here I am." "Do not come any closer," God said. "Take off your sandals, for the place where you are standing is holy ground." Then he said, "I am the God of your father, the God of Abraham, the God of Isaac and the God of Jacob." At this, Moses hid his face, because he was afraid to look at God.

—EXODUS 3:1–6

Worship involves sanctity.

Imagine what Moses must've been thinking as he came upon that burning bush. It started off as a mere curiosity, but when he heard God calling his name from inside the bush, he immediately answered. He didn't think it was a trick or some figment of his imagination—he responded with full recognition that the voice was indeed addressing him.

Then God sprung something interesting on him: Moses was standing on holy ground, face to burning face with the God of his fathers. And it scared Moses because, even though he'd grown up in the house of Pharaoh, he knew exactly what God was talking about.

This sort of thing didn't happen often in the Old Testament—God always had to be approached. People had to ready their hearts to worship him. They had to say, in essence, "Here I am, God, to worship you."

God is holy. God deserves our respect. Jesus may live inside our hearts, but we still must make a conscious decision to approach God when we worship him. We don't have to remove our sandals. We don't need the exhilarating appearance of a burning bush to be prompted to worship.

But we must turn our hearts toward God, stand against anything that may be holding us back, and say, "Here I am, God. Here I am. I have come to worship you, and that is what I shall do."

Prayer for the Day:

O, holy God. God of my fathers. God of Abraham, and of Isaac, and of Jacob. I am here to worship you. I worship you in song, I worship you in word, I worship you in deed. I worship you with my entire life. I am in the place you've put me so that I may worship you. I am in love with you, Jesus. I worship you.

AMEN.

DAY 11: Here I Am to Worship

In the year that King Uzziah died, I saw the Lord seated on a throne, high and exalted, and the train of his robe filled the temple. Above him were seraphs, each with six wings: With two wings they covered their faces, with two they covered their feet, and with two they were flying. And they were calling to one another: "Holy, holy, holy is the LORD Almighty; the whole earth is full of his glory." At the sound of their voices the doorposts and thresholds shook and the temple was filled with smoke. "Woe to me!" I cried. "I am ruined! For I am a man of unclean lips, and I *live among a people of unclean lips, and my eyes have seen the King, the LORD Almighty." Then one of the seraphs flew to me with a live coal in his hand, which he had taken with tongs from the altar. With it he touched my mouth and said, "See, this has touched your lips; your guilt is taken away and your sin atoned for." Then I heard the voice of the Lord saying, "Whom shall I send? And who will go for us?" And I said, "Here am I. Send me!"*

—ISAIAH 6:1–8

Worship involves service.

Years after Moses stood before the burning bush, Isaiah had a similar encounter with God and fire. And he, too, was afraid to see God—possibly for the same reason Moses was afraid. But Isaiah's situation was different, for he also encountered seraphs while he was singing praises to God—praises that shook the temple.

Isaiah knew this was a holy moment. And, realizing his uncleanness, he was filled with woe. He was unable to enjoy this moment of worship because of his guilt and the guilt of those who surrounded him in his everyday life. God immediately recognized Isaiah's situation and made a way for him to be sanctified.

Notice what Isaiah says as soon as God cleanses him. God asks who he should send, and Isaiah chimes in with, "Here am I. Send me!" Eager and willing to serve, Isaiah sought to worship God with his life and his service.

That is the attitude of worship we should have. We've been made clean! God has provided a way for us to approach him without fear, reservation, or guilt. The only appropriate response is, "Here we are, Lord. Send us! Send us wherever you want us to go!"

It is an honor and a joy to serve him.

Prayer for the Day:

God, you are holy and you are mighty. The earth is indeed filled with millions of examples of your glory. Lord, I am humbled that you've seen fit to cleanse me so that I can look upon you. I'm humbled that you allow me to worship you so closely. I'm humbled that you would ask me to serve you. God, I pray that you would give me an eagerness and willingness to serve you. May your will be done in my life.

AMEN.

DAY 12: Here I Am to Bow Down

King Nebuchadnezzar made an image of gold, ninety feet high and nine feet wide, and set it up on the plain of Dura in the province of Babylon. He then summoned the satraps, prefects, governors, advisers, treasurers, judges, magistrates and all the other provincial officials to come to the dedication of the image he had set up. So the satraps, prefects, governors, advisers, treasurers, judges, magistrates and all the other provincial officials assembled for the dedication of the image that King Nebuchadnezzar had set up, and they stood before it. Then the herald loudly proclaimed, "This is what you are commanded to do, O peoples, nations and men of every language: As soon as you hear the sound of the horn, flute, zither, lyre, harp, pipes and all kinds of music, you must fall down and worship the image of gold that King Nebuchadnezzar has set up. Whoever does not fall down and worship will immediately be thrown into a blazing furnace." ... Shadrach, Meshach and Abednego replied to the king, "O Nebuchadnezzar, we do not need to defend ourselves before you in this matter. If we are thrown into the blazing furnace, the God we serve is able to save us from it, and he will rescue us from your hand, O king. But even if he does not, we want you to know, O king, that we will not serve your gods or worship the image of gold you have set up."

—Daniel 3:1–6; 16–18

Worship involves commitment.

What a remarkable statement from Shadrach, Meshach, and Abednego. They were captives, stranded in a country that was not the country of their birth, yet they still retained their allegiance to God and found an audience with the king because of it. The king was furious with them for refusing to bow to the statue he set up, but they stood their ground in the face of certain death.

That's commitment. That's confidence in God. Commitment. No matter what, live or die, they refused to bow to anyone or anything other than God.

We, too, are called to bow to no one but God. In fact, there are people in the world right now who are being punished for refusing to bow their knee, literally and figuratively, to something other than God. There are martyrs in other countries who are not being saved from their own "blazing furnaces," but are instead being ushered into eternity because of their stance for the Lord.

We must treasure the freedom we have to bow to God and only him.

Prayer for the Day:

Lord God, I thank you for the freedom I have to bow to you. I pray that others across the world would get a chance to experience that freedom as well. Lord, there are so many things vying for my attention—give me the strength to resist them and to instead bow to you, Lord. I am here to bow down, and bow down I do.

AMEN.

DAY 13: Here I Am to Bow Down

Turn to me and be saved, all you ends of the earth; for I am God, and there is no other. By myself I have sworn, my mouth has uttered in all integrity a word that will not be revoked: Before me every knee will bow; by me every tongue will swear. They will say of me, "In the Lord alone are righteousness and strength." All who have raged against him will come to him and be put to shame. But in the Lord all the descendants of Israel will be found righteous and will exult.

—Isaiah 45:22–25

Worship involves humility.

We all want to be exalted in some way. When we do good things, we want to be recognized for it. We want to be able to stand proud, hold our heads high, and say, "Yes, I did that."

What we often forget, though, is that recognition comes through humility because God is the one who exalts us. Therefore, when we willfully bow our knees to him, he will raise us up in the way he sees fit.

Everyone will bow his or her knee to God at some point.

Everyone will call him the Lord of all creation. All the more reason for us to begin worshipping now by bowing our hearts to him and calling him Lord. There is power in our ability to bow.

When we bow, when we humble ourselves, we are telling God that we recognize we are powerless without him. It is our way of offering our lives to him, because without him our lives would have no meaning.

God is looking for humble hearts. Hearts that say, "Lord, I am here to bow down to you. Do with me what you will."

May we all bow.

Prayer for the Day:

I bow down, Lord. I bow my heart at your throne in worship and adoration, for you are too marvelous and awesome for me to remain on my feet. Lord, I pray that you will help me have a humble heart toward you. As I bow low, I pray that you will be the one to raise me up. Make me a standard among my peers. Help me to treat others with humility, so they might see you in me. Here I am, bowing down. I worship you, Father.

AMEN.

DAY 14: Here I Am to Say That You're My God

That if you confess with your mouth, "Jesus is Lord," and believe in your heart that God raised him from the dead, you will be saved. For it is with your heart that you believe and are justified, and it is with your mouth that you confess and are saved.

—ROMANS 10:9–10

Worship involves confession.

There are many potential gods in our society today. Money, the opposite sex, food, celebrities … the list goes on and on. All these things crave our attention and our worship. The Devil wants them to be our lord—as long as something other than Jesus is telling us what to do.

So if God is really our God, if Jesus is really our Lord, then how do we keep ourselves from falling into the snares of all these other potential gods? By saying it out loud. By confirming our decision with a confession from our own mouth.

There's just something about hearing yourself say, "Jesus, you're my Lord" that makes it more real. In addition to proclaiming it once more to Jesus himself, you're proclaiming it once more to your own spirit. When we say, "God, you are my God," we are reminding ourselves of our true affiliations … and reminding the Devil that we don't buy his lies.

Confession.

It isn't insinuation. It isn't circumstantial evidence. It is hands-down proof. When we confess that God is our God, we're telling the world—and ourselves—what we believe.

**God, you are indeed our God.
We confess it today.**

Prayer for the Day:

God, give me the boldness to use my tongue today for you. Help me to speak unapologetically about you. Help me to say that you are my God, no matter what the consequences may be. May my mouth worship you this day, and may the rest of my body, soul, and spirit follow suit.

AMEN.

DAY 15: Here I Am to Say That You're My God

Then Jesus told them, "This very night you will all fall away on account of me, for it is written: 'I will strike the shepherd, and the sheep of the flock will be scattered.' But after I have risen, I will go ahead of you into Galilee." Peter replied, "Even if all fall away on account of you, I never will." "I tell you the truth," Jesus answered, "this very night, before the rooster crows, you will disown me three times." But Peter declared, "Even if I have to die with you, I will never disown you." And all the other disciples said the same.

—MATTHEW 26:31–35

Worship involves relentless dedication.

Jesus knew Peter's heart. He knew Peter really did love him with a fervent love—the type of love that made promises Jesus knew wouldn't be kept. Peter had a relentless dedication to Jesus, so much so that he was the only disciple who rushed to defend his Master when soldiers came to arrest him in the Garden of Gethsemane.

But Peter's love, while earnest, was naïve enough to cause Peter to believe he could do anything. Peter's boast in this passage reveals that Peter was so bent on his dedication that he disregarded the words of Jesus. Jesus tells Peter to his face that he will disown his Master, and Peter actually has the audacity to tell Jesus he's wrong.

Peter thought he could stand strong, but Jesus' words came to fruition a few hours later when Peter did in fact disown Jesus three times in a row. The point? We need to be relentlessly dedicated to God, yes, but we need to be relentlessly dedicated to seeking his help as well.

God is your God. You are not. Nor is your small group. Or your pastor. Or your spouse.

We must say that he is our God, and that we need his help.

Prayer for the Day:

Lord God, I thank you that I have the opportunity and privilege to dedicate myself to you. I pray that you'll help me follow you no matter what. I can't do this on my own—I am not my own god. You are my God. I need your help to live a life that is pleasing to you. Thank you for blessing me with that help.

AMEN.

DAY 16:
You're Altogether Lovely

How lovely is your dwelling place, O LORD Almighty! My soul yearns, even faints, for the courts of the LORD; my heart and my flesh cry out for the living God.

—PSALM 84:1–2

Worship involves yearning.

How do you feel about God? Does your soul yearn and faint for his courts?

Do your heart and flesh cry out for him?

The psalmists who wrote this passage obviously had an abiding love for God that went beyond mere words. It was something they felt deep within themselves. Interestingly, this psalm is attributed to "the sons of Korah," a special choir that had one specific job: to worship God in the temple.

Here is a choir of people whose entire lives were dedicated to one thing: worshiping God.

And this is how they felt about him.

They spent all day in worship. For months. Years. But instead of growing tired of God, or maybe getting too familiar with the worship formula, they felt a yearning in their souls—just for God's courts! Their souls longed just to be in the same area as God!

It's all too easy for "worship" to become something far less than worship. It is easy to think of "worship" as the twenty or thirty minutes of singing we endure before the preaching. And maybe we clap and raise our hands a couple of times, and it all becomes rote.

But God is lovely. He is worth yearning for. Our hearts and our flesh cry out for him. Our worship experiences must extend beyond singing for twenty minutes once a week.

Our worship experiences must involve a constant yearning for God and his loveliness.

Prayer for the Day:

O Lord, you are lovely. You are so wonderful, God, and I pray that my soul would indeed begin to yearn for you. That my heart and flesh would cry out for you, O God. That I would come to the place where I crave more and more of your presence, Lord. May I never be satisfied.

AMEN.

DAY 17:
You're
Altogether
Lovely

Give thanks to the LORD, call on his name; make known among the nations what he has done. Sing to him, sing praise to him; tell of all his wonderful acts. Glory in his holy name; let the hearts of those who seek the LORD rejoice. Look to the LORD and his strength; seek his face always. Remember the wonders he has done, his miracles, and the judgments he pronounced, O descendants of Israel his servant, O sons of Jacob, his chosen ones.

—1 CHRONICLES 16:8–13

Worship involves remembrance.

God loves it when we remember the awesome things he has done, both in our present lives and throughout history. There is power in remembrance, in taking stock of the good things that have happened in the past. By remembering the times when God was good to us, when God saved us, and when God helped us in a dire situation, we can remind ourselves that if he did it once, he most certainly can do it again.

Remembrance is a commandment for a reason. Without memories of God and his wonders, we are living foundationless lives, making it all the easier to be knocked to and fro by the troubles of this world.

But memories form a firm foundation that offers strength when the storms of life come. Memories of God's wonders, miracles, and judgments are anchors that help us maintain perspective and stay on track.

We must always remember the lovely things of God, for he is lovely. And through that remembrance, we not only seek God's face, but we encourage others to seek him as well.

When we tell of his wonderful acts, we are spreading the news of God's goodness to all who would hear it, and that is worship indeed.

Prayer for the Day:

Dear Lord. Lovely, lovely Lord. Help me to remember those marvelous things you've done. Not just the things you've done for me, but for my friends and family. For my church. For the saints written about in your Word. God, help me to keep a firm grasp on your character by looking at your acts and remembering you. Especially, Jesus, help me to remember your death on the cross. I remember you, Lord. You're altogether lovely.

AMEN.

DAY 18: Altogether Worthy

Sing to the Lord, all the earth; proclaim his salvation day after day. Declare his glory among the nations, his marvelous deeds among all peoples. For great is the Lord and most worthy of praise; he is to be feared above all gods. For all the gods of the nations are idols, but the Lord made the heavens. Splendor and majesty are before him; strength and joy in his dwelling place. Ascribe to the Lord, O families of nations, ascribe to the Lord glory and strength, ascribe to the Lord the glory due his name. Bring an offering and come before him; worship the Lord in the splendor of his holiness. Tremble before him, all the earth! The world is firmly established; it cannot be moved. Let the heavens rejoice, let the earth be glad; let them say among the nations,

"The Lord reigns!" Let the sea resound, and all that is in it; let the fields be jubilant, and everything in them! Then the trees of the forest will sing, they will sing for joy before the Lord, for he comes to judge the earth.

—1 Chronicles 16:23–33

Worship involves an awesome God.

The passage above is, quite simply, breathtaking. David sang this song of praise upon seeing the ark of the covenant brought back into Jerusalem after it had been captured by the Philistines. David's song burst forth in gratitude and he composed this wonderful treatise on God's greatness.

And it fails to do him justice.

Our minds simply cannot fathom God's greatness. We cannot comprehend how truly awesome he is. But we can say, "You're altogether worthy." We can offer the simplest of comments.

Praise him for all he has done! He is wonderful! He reigns over all! He is just! He is great! He is glorious! He sets all creation singing!

And he cares about us.

This is the God of all creation, and he allows us to have an audience with him. He is mighty; the creator of all, yet he tells us to approach him in worship. He is altogether worthy. We are far from it.

How amazing that God cares for us the way he does. How worthy he is.

Prayer for the Day:

I am humbled, Lord, that you allow me to communicate with you. All your creation sings to you, and I am honored to be part of that creation song. Lord, you're worthy of my praise, and I offer it to you with a contrite heart. I pray you'll receive my praise in the spirit it is offered and smile upon it. I worship you, for you are worthy.

AMEN.

DAY 19: Altogether Worthy

The beginning of the gospel about Jesus Christ, the Son of God. It is written in Isaiah the prophet: "I will send my messenger ahead of you, who will prepare your way—a voice of one calling in the desert, 'Prepare the way for the Lord, make straight paths for him.'" And so John came, baptizing in the desert region and preaching a baptism of repentance for the forgiveness of sins. The whole Judean countryside and all the people of Jerusalem went out to him. Confessing their sins, they were baptized by him in the Jordan River. John wore clothing made of camel's hair, with a leather belt around his waist, and he ate locusts and wild honey. And this was his message: "After me will come one more powerful than I, the thongs of whose sandals I am not worthy to stoop down and untie. I baptize you with water, but he will baptize you with the Holy Spirit."

—MARK 1:1–8

Worship involves recognition of our place.

This passage very clearly states that John the Baptist's coming was prophesied by Isaiah. When he arrived, he became extraordinarily popular, so much so that virtually everyone in the region went to see him and hear what he had to say. They confessed their sins to him. They let him baptize them. John the Baptist was a powerful guy.

But next to Jesus, he was nothing.

And he said as much.

John the Baptist recognized that, despite all his fame and popularity and power, compared to Jesus, he was nothing. He wasn't even worthy to untie Jesus' shoes. That's pretty lowly.

When we recognize our true place, we are on the road to unique and honest worship. We are, in a sense, all called to be like John the Baptist. We are called to proclaim Jesus and the kingdom of God; but we should also remember that we are not worthy to untie Jesus' shoes.

On one hand, we're lifted up and exalted; on the other, we are humbled and bowed down.

The two essences of worship.

May we never forget our place in God's kingdom.

Prayer for the Day:

Father God, thank you for giving me a place in your kingdom. Thank you for letting me be your ambassador here on earth. Help me to recognize my place and position and to grow in it. I pray that you will give me the boldness and courage to proclaim your name as I go through my day, and I pray that you will help me to worship you in spirit and in truth. Thank you, Lord.

AMEN.

DAY 20: Altogether Wonderful to Me

The king went to Gibeon to offer sacrifices, for that was the most important high place, and Solomon offered a thousand burnt offerings on that altar. At Gibeon the LORD appeared to Solomon during the night in a dream, and God said, "Ask for whatever you want me to give you." Solomon answered, "You have shown great kindness to your servant, my father David, because he was faithful to you and righteous and upright in heart. You have continued this great kindness to him and have given him a son to sit on his throne this very day. Now, O LORD my God, you have made your servant king in place of my father David. But I am only a little child and do not know how to carry out my duties. Your servant is here among the people you have chosen, a great people, too numerous to count or number. So give your servant a discerning heart to govern your people and to distinguish between right and wrong. For who is able to govern this great people of yours?" The Lord was pleased that Solomon had asked for this. So God said to him, "Since you have asked for this and not for long life or wealth for yourself, nor have asked for the death of your enemies but for discernment in administering justice, I will do what you have asked. I will give you a wise and discerning heart, so that there will never have been anyone like you, nor will there ever be. Moreover, I will give you what you have not asked for—both riches and honor—so that in your lifetime you will have no equal among kings. And if you walk in my ways and obey my statutes and commands as David your father did, I will give you a long life."

—1 KINGS 3:4–14

Worship involves the desire to receive from God.

This passage references a great worship experience recorded in the Bible, as Solomon, whose throne had just been established, sought out God's face at the beginning of his rule.

Solomon's honest, lengthy worship resulted in a visit from God. We can presume that Solomon had been hoping to receive something from God, since he had an answer for the question God posed. He didn't go into that worship experience without a heart that was prepared to receive.

And receive he did. Solomon relied on his God-given wisdom for the rest of his life. But he never would have received it without initially worshipping God. Prior to his first sacrifice, did Solomon think, "I hope I get some wisdom out of this"? Perhaps. More than likely, though, he simply thought, "I hope I receive from God." Then, in the midst of worship, his heart began to align with God's heart, so that when God asked the question, Solomon immediately knew the best, most godly answer.

When we live lives of worship, we connect with God's heart, and in turn fill our hearts with godly desires.

May we receive.

Prayer for the Day:

Lord, I pray for an empty, open heart. A heart you can fill with your desires, not mine. I want to receive from you, Lord. You are so wonderful, God. I am amazed at your wonder, and I stand in awe of you. Thank you for looking in my direction. Thank you for filling me with godly desires.

AMEN.

DAY 21: Altogether Wonderful to Me

And without faith it is impossible to please God, because anyone who comes to him must believe that he exists and that he rewards those who earnestly seek him.

—HEBREWS 11:6

Worship involves faith.

Rewards are everywhere these days. Airline miles, restaurant gift certificates, portable music players … we are inundated with reward possibilities. Just buy this product, use this service, or fill out this survey to receive your reward.

God believes in rewards too. In fact, he thought up the whole idea of rewards.

The writer of Hebrews reminds us that God rewards those who seek him, but before we get to the reward, we must discover our faith. It is faith that leads to the reward; indeed, faith believes that the reward is even there.

We use our faith to pursue God, to seek him in earnest. And the Bible clearly states in this passage that when we do that, when we point our faith in the right direction, we will be rewarded.

So what's the reward? Certainly something more than a percent discount or "buy-one-get-one-free." Some may argue that God rewards with material blessings, which is certainly true, but isn't knowing God better reward enough? He is altogether wonderful, and he calls us friends.

That is some reward.

Prayer for the Day:

Lord, I pray for the faith that it takes to seek you in earnest. I know that you reward those who seek you, and I want to be a reward-worthy seeker. I want to know you and your wonderful ways more and more each day. God, I also want to have the faith to trust that you'll reward me in due time and in due fashion. Thank you for being so wonderful to me. I love you.

AMEN.

DAY 22: King of All Days

In the sixth month, God sent the angel Gabriel to Nazareth, a town in Galilee, to a virgin pledged to be married to a man named Joseph, a descendant of David. The virgin's name was Mary. The angel went to her and said, "Greetings, you who are highly favored! The Lord is with you." Mary was greatly troubled at his words and wondered what kind of greeting this might be. But the angel said to her, "Do not be afraid, Mary, you have found favor with God. You will be with child and give birth to a son, and you are to give him the name Jesus. He will be great and will be called the Son of the Most High. The Lord God will give him the throne of his father David, and he will reign over the house of Jacob forever; his kingdom will never end."

—LUKE 1:26–33

Worship involves trembling.

Let's imagine for a moment what Mary must have been feeling when Gabriel appeared to her. Here she was, an ordinary Jewish girl pledged to be married, living a normal life.

And then an angel shows up and starts telling her how favored she is with God. A little unsettling, perhaps. Mary was troubled at the angel's appearing, which is certainly an appropriate response. And on top of her troubles, she wondered what he was talking about.

But the angel is quick to put her fears to rest and give her the good news. She's going to give birth to a king whose kingdom will never end!

He will be the king of all days.

How wonderful it must've been for Mary to receive that news. How she must have trembled with awe, excitement, and maybe a little nervousness upon learning her destiny. She would be the first to worship the king.

Jesus' kingdom will never end. How wonderful it is that we get to serve him! Like Mary, we should tremble before the king of all days with awe, excitement, and maybe a little nervousness.

We are in the king's employ, and we should tremble before him.

Prayer for the Day:

Jesus, king of all days, I tremble before your throne. I'm excited about the calling you have for my life, and I'm in awe that I actually get to serve you. Thank you for the hope I have in your never-ending kingdom. I will worship you—and only you—forever. I love you and adore you.

AMEN.

DAY 23:
King of All Days

God, the blessed and only Ruler, the King of kings and Lord of lords, who alone is immortal and who lives in unapproachable light, whom no one has seen or can see. To him be honor and might forever. Amen.

—1 TIMOTHY 6:15B–16

Worship involves honor.

Consider for a moment the president of the United States. He is not a man who can just be approached out of the blue. None of us will ever bump into him alone on the street and get a handshake or an autograph.

No, the president must be approached with a sense of honor. And whether we individually agree with his politics or not, we'd still treat him with honor were we given the chance to meet him. Why? Because he's the leader of our country and a very powerful man.

So what about God?

God's authority supercedes that of the president. How should we approach him?

With honor.

He is the king of all days. He deserves our

honor and praise. Yes, he is our Father, and yes, he calls us friend, but he must also be honored above all others for he alone is immortal and he lives in unapproachable light.

He allows us the dignity of approaching him. The least we can do is approach him with the proper honor.

Prayer for the Day:

Lord, I honor you. Thank you for establishing a relationship with me, for reaching down from your throne and seeking me out. My prayer this day is that I would honor your kingship in my every action. I pray that you would give me the ability to show honor to you and to all your creation, especially my fellow humans. May I be a good emissary on your behalf. Thank you, Lord.

AMEN.

DAY 24: Oh So Highly Exalted

This is why it says: "When he ascended on high, he led captives in his train and gave gifts to men." (What does "he ascended" mean except that he also descended to the lower, earthly regions? He who descended is the very one who ascended higher than all the heavens, in order to fill the whole universe.)

—EPHESIANS 4:8–10

Worship involves looking up.

Jesus' time during the crucifixion drove him to a point lower than any other person has endured. His beatings, his torturous walk to Golgotha, his time on the cross … all these drove him lower and lower.

And when he died, he went lower still. All the way to hell.

Jesus' final hours on earth and first hours after death were one continuous descent—on purpose. He purposely descended into the lower, earthly regions to defeat death. He defeated hell. He defeated the Devil.

And then he rose. And rose. And rose. And ascended higher than all the heavens to the point of filling the entire universe.

Jesus' descent made his ascent all the more dramatic. He is higher than all else. And yet he loves us and seeks a relationship with us!

When Jesus ascended, he proclaimed victory for those who would seek to follow him. He gave us all a reason to hold our heads high. We needn't look down, for he isn't there. He ascended on high. We need to look up.

**We need to be expectant. Confident.
He obtained victory for us.
Look up.**

Prayer for the Day:

Dear Jesus, first and foremost, thank you for your sacrifice on the cross. Thank you for giving up your life so that I might have it. Thank you for winning the victory over death on my behalf, and for ascending up into glory. Help me to hold my head up and walk in the confidence and victory you've achieved for me. I pray that as I look up, you would look down on me.

AMEN.

DAY 25:
Glorious in Heaven Above

Your attitude should be the same as that of Christ Jesus: Who, being in very nature God, did not consider equality with God something to be grasped, but made himself nothing, taking the very nature of a servant, being made in human likeness. And being found in appearance as a man, he humbled himself and became obedient to death—even death on a cross! Therefore God exalted him to the highest place and gave him the name that is above every name, that at the name of Jesus every knee should bow, in heaven and on earth and under the earth, and every tongue confess that Jesus Christ is Lord, to the glory of God the Father.

—**PHILIPPIANS 2:5–11**

Worship involves imitation.

Imitation, as the old saying goes, is the sincerest form of flattery. Flattery by definition is insincere, but imitation isn't. We imitate those people whom we admire or respect, hoping that by imitating their behavior, we can become a little bit like them. We attempt to incorporate a little of them into our lives.

In this passage, the apostle Paul admonishes us to imitate Christ. There really is no one better to imitate. Christ, who had spent all eternity in the glorious heavens, defied all human comprehension and became nothing in obedience to God the Father. He even humbled himself to the point of dying on a cross, one of the lowliest, least honorable forms of death in the world.

And he never complained. Not once.

No one had a better reason to complain than Jesus—who was taken from the highest position possible and sent into this very earth so he could die. But Christ willingly accepted God's call and ... what happened? He became exalted.

Exaltation through humility is Christ's example. We would all do well to follow it.

Prayer for the Day:

Jesus, thank you for accepting the call of the Father. Thank you for humbling yourself to enter this world and take on human form. Thank you for humbling yourself even further by dying on the cross. I pray that you would enable me to follow your example. Help me obey you, no matter what the cost. Help me to obey you without grumbling or complaining, because you didn't. Thank you, Jesus, for victory.

AMEN.

DAY 26: Humbly You Came to the Earth You Created

So Joseph also went up from the town of Nazareth in Galilee to Judea, to Bethlehem the town of David, because he belonged to the house and line of David. He went there to register with Mary, who was pledged to be married to him and was expecting a child. While they were there, the time came for the baby to be born, and she gave birth to her firstborn, a son. She wrapped him in cloths and placed him in a manger, because there was no room for them in the inn.

—LUKE 2:4–7

Worship involves making room for the humble visitation of Christ.

What a humble way to enter this world. Bethlehem must've been a crowded, crowded place at the time Jesus was born, because his parents couldn't find a room anywhere. Every inn was full, apparently, and nobody wanted to make room for them.

So they stayed in a stable, more than likely not the nicest of places. Drafty, smelly, noisy—it was a far cry from a comfortable inn. Nevertheless, that's where the king of all days was born. That's where Jesus entered the world.

God could've made sure that Jesus found a more comfortable, opulent way to enter this world, but God wouldn't send Jesus anywhere he wasn't wanted. If the innkeeper didn't want to make room for Jesus, God certainly wasn't going to force him to accept the Savior of mankind.

We, too, must make room for the humble visitation of Christ. He will not wedge his way into our hearts uninvited. Instead he goes where he is wanted. That's why it's imperative that, in our worship, we open up our hearts for his warm, humble presence.

Best of all, if Jesus would go into a mucky stable as a newborn baby, there is no amount of uncleanness in our hearts that would prevent him from entering.

It doesn't matter what kind of room we make, as long as we make it.

Prayer for the Day:

*Lord, I open my heart today and ask you to
fill it. I make a point to empty selfishness from
my heart so you can have room in it. Please
help me to have your humility, and please
enable me to make even more room for you.
Thank you, Lord.*

AMEN.

DAY 27:
All for Love's Sake Became Poor

For you know the grace of our Lord Jesus Christ, that though he was rich, yet for your sakes he became poor, so that you through his poverty might become rich.

—2 CORINTHIANS 8:9

Worship involves grace.

Unbelievable, but true. Jesus took poverty upon himself in order to give us richness. But what sort of riches? When someone mentions the word "riches," we tend to automatically conjure up images of buried treasure chests or piles of gold coins hidden in a cave somewhere.

But when Jesus became poor for our sakes, was he really trying to help us become rich in the materialistic sense? Was Jesus' sacrifice on the cross simply the World's Greatest Success Seminar? Was it Jesus' aim to give us a life of lavish luxury? Probably not.

Jesus gave us true riches.

He took on the spiritual poverty that is sin so that we might enjoy a richer life with him. Our lives of servitude for Jesus are richer than our lives of slavery to sin. Through his sacrifice, we can cast off the poverty of sin and live richly.

But we must accept his grace to do it. We can do that through worship. When we worship, we turn our hearts toward Jesus and accept the riches he has to offer. We accept his grace.

We become rich.

Prayer for the Day:

Almighty God, I thank you for taking on my spiritual poverty so that I might experience your spiritual riches. I pray that you'll help me to make the most of the rich life you offer, and that you'll infuse me with your grace where I need it. Help me to accept your riches, despite my lowly stature. Show me how to share your grace with others today. In your name I pray.

AMEN.

DAY 28: All for Love's Sake Became Poor

Let us fix our eyes on Jesus, the author and perfecter of our faith, who for the joy set before him endured the cross, scorning its shame, and sat down at the right hand of the throne of God.

Consider him who endured such opposition from sinful men, so that you will not grow weary and lose heart.

Worship involves joy.

The sweat. The blood. The pain. The agony. The piercing of the thorns. The splintery wood. The aching muscles. The popping joints.

Jeers. Taunts. Scorn. Mockery.

Jesus endured it all. He knew when he came to this earth that the cross would be torture, but he did it anyway. He lasted through the entire experience because he knew the joy that would be on the other side of it.

That joy outweighed the pain of the crucifixion.

Hard to believe, but true.

And that joy is available to us as believers. It is there for us when we encounter scorn and ridicule from an overbearing boss. It is there for us when we find ourselves enduring financial hardships. It is there for us when our children are rebelling against us. It is there for us when a loved one dies.

Joy.

The joy of what is to come carried Christ through the crucifixion. If it can do that, it is more than capable of carrying us through anything we might have to face.

Let us set our eyes on the joy that is to come!

Prayer for the Day:

Jesus, I'm so thankful that you set your eyes on joy. I'm so thankful that you endured what you went through. As I look out upon the hardships I'm faced with today, I pray that you'll help me look past them and see the joy that awaits me, just like you did when you went to the cross. Thank you for an infusion of joy in my life today!

AMEN.

DAY 29:
I'll Never Know How Much It Cost

Surely he took up our infirmities and carried our sorrows, yet we considered him stricken by God, smitten by him, and afflicted. But he was pierced for our transgressions, he was crushed for our iniquities; the punishment that brought us peace was upon him, and by his wounds we are healed. We all, like sheep, have gone astray, each of us has turned to his own way; and the Lord has laid on him the iniquity of us all.

—Isaiah 53:4–6

Greater love has no one than this, that he lay down his life for his friends.

—John 15:13

Worship involves Jesus' sacrifice.

There is often a lot of talk about sacrifice in our world today. There are sacrifices in baseball, sacrifices at the office, financial sacrifices … sacrifices run the gamut from the mundane to the important.

But there is one sacrifice in history that outshines them all as the greatest sacrifice ever. There is no greater love than someone laying down his life for his friends, and no greater sacrifice than Jesus demonstrating his love for us by laying down his life on the cross.

Even greater still—Isaiah the prophet declared that "we considered him stricken by God, smitten by him, and afflicted." In other words, no one knew the real reason for Jesus' death when he died, but he went through with it anyway.

Amazing. That is true sacrifice.

Jesus was crucified, and the disciples, the government, the people watching—everyone thought it was for a reason other than the true one. No one saw it coming. Despite the prophecies that pointed toward Jesus, no one knew the real reason he'd come to earth.

This includes the Devil. He was totally flummoxed. And Jesus defeated him through his sacrifice.

We can never know the actual cost Jesus paid to do that. But we can be thankful for it. And we can worship him for it.

Prayer for the Day:

*Jesus, I don't understand your ways some-
times. I don't understand how you endured
what you endured, and I admit right now that
I don't comprehend what it took for you to lay
down your life for me. Thank you for loving
me that much, Jesus. I am only able to worship you because you loved me that much.
Thank you. Thank you. Thank you.*

AMEN.

DAY 30:
To See My Sin upon That Cross

When you were dead in your sins and in the uncircumcision of your sinful nature, God made you alive with Christ. He forgave us all our sins, having canceled the written code, with its regula-

tions, that was against us and that stood opposed to us; he took it away, nailing it to the cross. And having disarmed the powers and authorities, he made a public spectacle of them, triumphing over them by the cross.

—COLOSSIANS 2:13–15

Worship involves triumph!

Remember the 2004 Boston Red Sox? It was an astonishing story of underdog determination during the playoffs as the Red Sox fell behind the New York Yankees three games to nothing in a best of seven series. In order to make it to the World Series, the Red Sox had to win four games in a row.

And they did it.

Then they got to the World Series and dominated the St. Louis Cardinals to become World Series Champions for the first time in decades. Triumph at last! Victory!

It was the biggest sports story of the year—maybe of the decade. The amazing come-from-behind win by a team that never could get their act together enough to win the big game.

In comparison to Jesus' victory, that World Series win is so minuscule as to require a microscope.

We were dead in sin, and Jesus took that sin away by nailing it to the cross. Christ died, but rose again, and now God says we are alive with him!

And best of all—when Jesus died and rose again, he exposed sin and death for what they really are: defeated by the cross. Jesus came and illuminated those dark places, eliminating their power over mankind. He triumphed! He is the true victor!

We have a greater victory than any world championship. Let us celebrate it in worship!

Prayer for the Day:

Jesus, thank you so much for winning the victory! I am shocked and amazed at your goodness to me, and I thank you so much that you allow me to participate in the triumph you won over sin and death. Help me to walk in victory this day, and help me to have a worshipful attitude toward you. You are alive! You are victorious! I worship you.

AMEN.

Additional copies of this and other Honor products

are available wherever good books are sold.

If you have enjoyed this book,

or if it has had an impact on your life,

we would like to hear from you.

Please contact us at:

Honor Books

Cook Communications Ministries, Dept. 201

4050 Lee Vance View

Colorado Springs, CO 80918

Or visit our Web site:

www.cookministries.com